Dressing floors at Hexworthy Mine, which was worked until 1920

The Making of
Modern Dartmoor

HELEN HARRIS

Bossiney Books · Lau

Merrivale, where this bridge on the turnpike road is now bypassed

Some other Bossiney titles which may be of interest

About Dartmoor
Ancient Dartmoor
Medieval Dartmoor
Ponies on Dartmoor

First published 2003 by
Bossiney Books Ltd, Langore, Launceston, Cornwall PL15 8LD
www.bossineybooks.co.uk

ISBN 1-899383-54-9

Acknowledgements
The map on page 32 is by Graham Hallowell.
The photographs on pages 24 and 25 are Crown copyright.
The photograph on page 26 is from the Beaford Photographic Archive.
Other photographs are by Paul White.
Printed in Great Britain by R Booth (Troutbeck Press), Mabe, Cornwall

Communications

Although looking timeless, the Dartmoor we see today has sustained many changes over the past 250 years. From the mid-18th century even this remote upland was affected by the great industrial revolution and by the advances in agriculture that were apparent elsewhere in the country. A growing national population called for both food and raw materials, and consequently for the means of transporting them.

While recognised trackways across the moor had existed for many centuries, better roads became necessary as more wheeled traffic ventured upon the scene. This was the era of turnpike roads, their construction empowered by Acts of Parliament and financed by loans from landowners and businessmen who then received tolls levied at toll-gates or 'turnpikes'.

A system of turnpikes encircling the moor was already mainly established when a cross-Dartmoor route was authorised in 1772. This comprised the road from Tavistock eastwards to Two Bridges and the north-easterly continuation to Moretonhampstead, plus a little over 3km from Two Bridges towards Ashburton. Easing gradients was a primary objective, which sometimes resulted in sharp bends that benefited horse-drawn vehicles more than modern traffic.

New bridges were necessary, including one close to the ancient clapper bridge at Postbridge crossing the East Dart, and there were toll-gates at Merrivale, Rundlestone, Postbridge and west of Moretonhampstead. In 1812 a further route on to the moor was established by the turnpike from Roborough Down on the south-west, which joined the earlier road at Two Bridges. The solid stone roads (not, of course, tarred in those days) greatly facilitated transport.

Conveyance of products from the growing extractive industries, however, was sometimes achieved by other means: horse-drawn tramways served quarries and peatworks even before Devon had any actual railways. It was not until the mid-19th century that the first railway arrived in the county, reaching Exeter in 1844 and Plymouth in 1848.

Travel was also helped by branch lines and by the addition of a northern railway around the moor to Plymouth. With better roads as well, visitors inevitably began to recognise and appreciate the moorland delights. Dartmoor was designated as a National Park in 1951, with a mandate to preserve and enhance natural beauty, and to encourage public enjoyment.

One of the great excavated gullies or 'beams' which form part of the Birch Tor & Vitifer mine near the Warren House Inn. The whole area between the Warren House Inn and Headland Warren Farm is full of such massive man-made valleys

Mining

Dartmoor was an area of much tin working from the 12th century onwards, but activities were greatly reduced from the late 1600s until the developments of the Industrial Revolution and keen demand for metals encouraged fresh prospecting.

Tin-dressing floors at Hooten Wheals, at the mine also known as Hensroost or Hexworthy. These buddles were built as late as 1905

While earlier workings were mainly surface or shallow, this later period involved true mining. With the benefit of new equipment and techniques, reserves at deeper levels could be exploited.

Tin production was low, however, compared with medieval levels, and sporadic, depending on fluctuating prices. Often, instead of vertical shafts, 'adits' were cut near-horizontally into hillsides to reach the lodes and also to drain water. Such was the case at Vitifer and Birch Tor mines (near the Warren House Inn, a convenient refreshment point for miners) which were worked from the late 18th century to around 1870 and between 1900 and the 1930s. Here, where slopes are scarred by huge openwork gullies originating from earlier work, in the valley below there are remains of leats (man-made watercourses) for powering waterwheels and ore-dressing machinery, wheelpits, routes to buildings, and tramways – all now largely reclaimed by nature.

Another of the last tin-mining areas was near Hexworthy, south of the road from the Forest Inn to Holne. On this site of earlier open works, mines were operated from the mid-19th century and latterly between 1900 and 1919.

The later stage saw modernisation in 1907: electrical power was generated by a Pelton wheel housed beside the road at Saddle Bridge (SX664719). Remains of the 1900s ore processing plant, as well as those of buildings and the earlier water powered system, are at SX661711-650713 and 655708.

Tin was also produced at other mines during the 1800s. Smelting on the moor ended in the early 19th century and dressed ore was then sent away unsmelted as 'black tin'.

Other metals were worked on the moorland fringes. Foremost of these was copper, worked notably at Wheal Friendship at Mary Tavy (SX508794). Production of copper (and lead) began here around 1714 and was re-started in 1746. Deepest workings were to 220 fathoms (1 fathom = 1.83 m). Copper production ceased in the 1870s but arsenic was later recovered from the waste.

Another large copper mine was Ramsley, at Sticklepath (SX650930), which opened in 1850 and last worked in 1909. Its old chimney stack surmounts the hill.

The best known example of lead mining is on Black Down, Mary Tavy, where the evocative Cornish engine house of Wheal Betsy (SX510812) stands near the road, preserved by The National Trust as a memorial to Dartmoor miners. The mine was re-opened in 1806 and also produced other minerals including silver. It closed in 1877.

Wheal Betsy engine house

Above: 'Feather and tare' marks on an unfinished block

Below: At around SX545755 are the remains of small, primitive workbenches called 'sett-makers' bankers'. Each consists of two upright pieces of granite almost half a metre apart, set into the hillside slope, with another slab across the top about a third of a metre above ground level. They may be spotted by the tell-tale presence of granite chips. The men crouched or knelt at their work, cutting the small setts from larger slabs. After Merrivale quarry was established, this work was done within its shelter

Granite working

Granite, the rock of which Dartmoor is formed, has been used from prehistoric times for building and for making items such as troughs and gateposts. Taking was permitted for those with commoners' rights and use was almost exclusively local. But around 1800, as towns developed and demands grew for construction and street paving, granite working became a more commercial venture.

Most of Dartmoor's commons were worked over as sources of loose, surface granite. Often one comes across large slabs displaying a line of half-round holes which indicate that they must have been split by a process known as 'feather-and-tare'. This involved making holes

Haytor Quarry, here visited by a school party pond-dipping

with a tool called a 'jumper', into each of which two curved metal 'feathers' were inserted to support the metal wedge or 'tare'. The tares were struck in turn with a sledge-hammer until the rock split. Dating from about 1800, the process is still used today, the jumpers being replaced by a power drill.

An area much worked for surface granite during the 19th century is that around Pew Tor and Staple Tor, on the western side of the moor. During the 1870s a need grew for street paving, notably in Plymouth, and the cutting of granite 'setts' for this purpose was an industrious activity, particularly on Staple Tor's eastern slopes.

Quarrying of granite began around 1780, leading to sizeable developments from about 1820. Good quality material had already been extracted on Haytor Down, and carried away by horses and carts, when George Templer of Stover won a contract for supplying granite for rebuilding London Bridge.

The opening of Haytor Quarry (SX755755) called for an improved means of transport which presented a problem, the quarry being about 400 m above sea level. This was solved by the construction of a

13.7 km tramway to connect with the Stover Canal (also owned by Templer), leading to the Teign estuary. Inaugurated in 1820, the 4 ft 1 in gauge 'rails' were of granite. At junctions of branches grooves were cut in the blocks to form 'points' which, when fitted with a special device, enabled alternative lines to be taken. The horse-drawn wagons assembled in 'trains' had flangeless wheels, and 'shoes' or chains probably aided braking.

Towards 1858 production at Haytor Quarry dwindled, and use of the tramway ceased. The impressive former main quarry and associated quarries are now quiet and often deserted.

Farther west on the moor and just west of Princetown on Walkhampton Common, where stone was extracted in the late 18th

The Haytor tramway. Its route on the down, which can still be followed, is scheduled as an ancient monument.

The granite blocks were roughly 1 ft (30 cm) square in section, cut to give a rebate 7½ in (19 cm) wide and 3 in (7.5 cm) deep, forming a longitudinal flange.

At junctions like the one in the photograph, grooves were cut out in the blocks to form 'points'. The small hole in the foreground was used for a hinged device which switched between branch-lines

century for the village's development, large quarries were started around 1820. They comprised: Foggintor (SX567736), King Tor (SX554739) and Swell Tor (SX560733). These, too, are all impressive and evocative of past working. They were also provided with a horse-drawn railway, to Plymouth – the Plymouth & Dartmoor Railway. It was completed to King Tor in 1823 and to Princetown in 1826.

Although 41 km long, the ascending, meandering route covered a direct distance of only about 21 km. The 4 ft 6 in gauge cast-iron rails were laid in cast-iron chairs to which they were bolted and then fixed to granite blocks. (Latterly, to reduce costs, chairs were dispensed with and, instead, large spikes were driven into the stone.)

By mid century the railway became disused (later it was reconstructed as the Princetown Railway – see page 27), but the quarries continued until the early 20th century. A notable product of Foggintor is Nelson's Column in London's Trafalgar Square.

Merrivale Quarry (SX546753) was developed from 1874 and worked into modern times, eventually closing in 1997. Cut and prepared in the 1980s, the War Memorial in the Falkland Islands came from here. Other smaller granite quarries abound on the moor.

Route of the Plymouth & Dartmoor Railway, not far from Princetown

Just part of an active china clay pit on southern Dartmoor

China clay

The working of china clay is still an active industry in the south-western area of Dartmoor; huge white pits and large waste dumps – many of them now grass-covered – provide prominent evidence.

China clay, or kaolin, is a derivative of granite. It was created by the decomposition of feldspar particles, leaving the other constituents – quartz and mica – unchanged. Working of the mineral, which began in Cornwall in the 18th century to meet demands from the English potteries, started on Lee Moor on Dartmoor in 1830. It quickly advanced with the making of fire bricks and glazed pipes. Many Cornishmen came to work here and so the village of Lee Moor was established. By 1870 there were nine separate clay works – the area of working lies in the parishes of Shaugh Prior and Cornwood, from Cadover Bridge to Shaugh Moor, Crownhill Down and Heddon Down.

Clay is extracted from pits by powerful streams of water and is carried in suspension to settling tanks where the heavier sand and mica particles separate out. The small clay particles then pass on to further tanks where, as they settle, water is drawn off. When dry enough, the clay residue is cut out and subjected to further drying. The modern works lie in the valley south of Lee Moor and Wotter. Most of their output is used in the paper industry, for filling and gloss; the rest finds its way into many other products, such as ceramics. A problem of the extraction is the disposal of waste constituents; this has resulted in massive 'artificial hills', some of which are seen from the Beatland Corner to Cornwood road.

From the 1850s to the 1930s the Lee Moor Tramway carried clay down to Plymouth's Cattewater quays. Of 4 ft 6 in gauge, over its life it used three forms of motive power: horse, gravity, and steam.

Remains of another clay treatment works can be seen near the River Avon at Shipley Bridge (SX 681629), near South Brent. On the hillside are rectangular and circular pits, and by the bridge is a building where the final solidifying was done. Clay was carried here in suspension from workings on Brent Moor in the 1850s and 1870s. Later there were further clay works at Redlake and Leftlake (north of Ugborough, SX 646668 and 647634). These were worked between 1910 and 1932, and were served by the 12 km, 3 ft gauge Redlake Mineral Railway, which connected with the Great Western Railway at Cantrell, Bittaford. Powered by a locomotive, it carried coal and goods, not clay, which was piped in suspension to the Cantrell works.

The remains of a long-abandoned drying works still to be seen south of the River Plym at Shaugh Bridge (SX 534636)

Route of the Rattlebrook Peat Railway

Peat

Another Dartmoor resource, peat, has been exploited commercially to a limited extent in modern times. Peat, which blankets much of the moor, is formed by the decomposition of plant material in saturated conditions, and occurs mainly on higher areas where wet ground, moist air and cool temperatures prevail together. It was used for fuel in early ages and in the time of the tinners, and in subsequent centuries by moor dwellers, its cutting being regular work for those holding appropriate rights.

In the 1840s peat cut near Fice's Well (SX 576758) was carried by horse tramway south to a naphtha works at Princetown. Another naphtha works, at Shipley Bridge (SX 681629) – later used by the clayworks (see page 12) – was supplied with peat from Redlake and transported on the Zeal Tor Tramway. Both survived only briefly. More ambitious was the Rattlebrook Peatworks (SX 559872) high on the moor, north-east of Lydford. Work started here around 1850, and over a century a succession of ventures aimed at producing fuel by hydraulic compression, and at extracting gas and even oil were tried. An 8 km 4ft 8 1/2 in gauge railway (horse, and later locomotive drawn) descended 290 m to connect with the main line at Bridestowe.

The Powder Mills

The abundance of Dartmoor water has long been utilised for powering waterwheels. As already noted, tinners used water power, while mills for grinding corn have existed in the area for centuries. Also, around the moor's fringes, there were mills for wool, metal tools, and paper.

Mills of a more unusual kind, the Powder Mills, were located in the heart of the moor between Two Bridges and Postbridge (SX 627774). Here gunpowder or 'black powder' – mainly used in quarrying – was manufactured between 1844 and the 1890s. The isolation was an advantage in handling such an explosive substance, and for the same reason the mill buildings were set apart from each other (explosions, with roofs being blown off, were not unusual!).

The process involved grinding and processing the ingredients – saltpetre (potassium nitrate), sulphur and charcoal – then combining and drying them. Water power was provided by leats, the buildings being served in succession. Flues and two chimney stacks carried fumes from the drying well away from the mill buildings.

At times a hundred men were employed, and various ancillary buildings included a cooperage for making barrels, a school, a chapel, and dwellings, some of which have been renovated for modern uses as houses and workshops.

Opposite: The Powder Mills

Enclosure walls near Princetown, probably dating from the early nineteenth century

Agriculture

In the latter half of the 18th century developments in agriculture – in both crop husbandry and livestock breeding – were advancing all over the country. Dartmoor did not escape the attention of individuals fired with optimism who considered that what some saw as a barren wilderness was capable of great improvement and potential prosperity.

Farming has, of course, been practised on Dartmoor from prehistoric times, but the schemes of the 'improvers' were intended to raise production to a higher plane. For centuries holders of ancient tenements had been allowed at certain times to enclose a 'newtake' of up to 8 acres (3.25 hectares). This privilege ended in 1796 when larger newtakes began appearing on the moor. They were bounded by dry stone walls, taken in under grant from the Duchy of Cornwall and supported by Act of Parliament.

Around 1780 the pioneer at Prince Hall (SX625743) was a Mr Gullett; several others followed. A notable enthusiast was Mr (later Sir) Thomas Tyrwhitt, friend of the Prince of Wales (later George IV) with whose backing he was able to establish Tor Royal (SX600731). (Tyrwhitt also founded Princetown – see page 21). He enclosed a large acreage and spent considerable sums on cultivation.

Most of the substantial granite walls around the Two Bridges area date from this time. However, the number of such enclosures were being reduced, and the process was stopped in the late 1800s. Success with crops was in any case limited due to the harsh natural conditions and short growing season.

Numerous other more modest small-holding ventures also began in the 19th century at points across the moor, although many of them have long since been abandoned. The last was Nun's Cross Farm (SX606698), south of Princetown, established by John Hooper around 1870.

Livestock kept on the moor has changed too. Up to the 19th century most of the moor was used as summer grazing ground only. South Devon type cattle, owned by farmers with rights, grazed it from May to October and were taken down to the lowland for winter. Similarly, flocks of the traditional long-wool breeds of sheep – white-faced 'Widecombe' Dartmoor on the east, and grey-faced Dartmoor on the west and north – grazed in summer and spent winter down in the 'in-country'.

The 'improvers' brought in other breeds: Galloway cattle (black, dun, and white in colour) and Scottish Black-face sheep. Such breeds can out-winter on the moor and, with crosses, predominate today.

Life for farming people on Dartmoor has always been rigorous. The nature of the land, the high rainfall, and sometimes long spells of winter snow call for toughness of spirit and the ability to cope in isolation. At least up to the First World War many Dartmoor farms relied on burning peat or wood in an open hearth for warmth and cooking and for scalding milk to produce clotted cream (used for making butter). Candles provided lighting. Gradually coal became more easily accessible for firing a range, and oil and bottled gas for lamps and burners for cooking brought another advance. Not until 1962 did all parishes on Dartmoor have mains electricity – Widecombe was the last to be connected.

Ditsworthy Warren Farm, near Drizzlecombe, where the warren had existed since ancient times, possibly since the twelfth century.

The farm was abandoned in the twentieth century as were many other farms on the high moorland – some of them after little more than a century of occupation

Since the Second World War modern technological developments have brought great changes to Dartmoor farmers and their families, in general comfort, in transport and the variety of vehicles available, and in communications systems. Nevertheless, the questionable state of future markets and economic uncertainties can still obscure the outlook and add a few imaginary clouds to the real ones that so often envelop the moor.

This stone row (with cist and cairn) at Lakehead Hill lies within the Bellever plantation, and is normally surrounded by conifers only a few metres away; but from time to time they are felled, and the Bronze Age monument can be seen properly

Forestry

Plantations of conifer trees began appearing on Dartmoor from the end of the 18th century. Attempts were made by 'improvers' using Scots pine and other softwood varieties and a few hardwoods, but mostly without much success. From the 1860s landowners established new woodlands around the moorland fringes and on the moor itself.

Following the First World War, when national timber resources became depleted, the Forestry Commission was created and certain areas were systematically planted with conifers. These were mainly at Fernworthy near Chagford, Beardown near Princetown, and Brimpts near Dartmeet. In the 1920s plantings were carried out at Bellever near Postbridge, and in the area of Burrator Reservoir by Plymouth Corporation. After the Second World War the Soussons plantation (between Postbridge and Widecombe) was established, and some of the earlier ones were enlarged.

Since then felling and replanting have been carried out as necessary, and now forests and woodlands occupy about 9 per cent of Dartmoor. While it is acknowledged that conifer plantations produce economically beneficial timber and provide enjoyable recreation, they also have a number of disadvantages: they reduce grazing land, obscure features of archaeological interest, and introduce a forbidding, dark and dominating element to an otherwise clear and open landscape. One of the Dartmoor National Park Authority's objectives is to modify some of the boundaries of afforestation to give less of a solid edge effect.

The National Park also encourages and assists in the establishment of small areas of hardwood planting at suitable locations, often near moorland villages.

The view from Bellever Tor

For contrast, some natural Dartmoor woodland – stunted oaks growing at the top of the Dewerstone cliffs

Ponies

The sight of ponies grazing on Dartmoor is attractive and appealing, especially when there are young foals around. Those of the Dartmoor breed are descended from wild ponies that inhabited the area from ancient times. Now, however, they are not wild in the sense of being 'un-owned'; all of them belong to farmers.

The true Dartmoor pony measures 11-12 hands and is noted for its hardiness. Able to withstand winter conditions, mares can produce and rear a foal in spring and regain full condition by summer. The ponies are of various colours: brown, bay, black, chestnut, grey or roan, and today uncharacteristic piebald or skewbald markings are often seen as well. These are the result of mixed breeding.

In the past ponies were sold for use in mines, for drawing small carts, and for children's riding. More recently most went to continental countries for meat. Now, though, there is practically no commercial market for the majority, and values have fallen to only a few pence. Steps are being taken, however, to restore the quality of the true breed, for which reasonable prices are obtainable.

Visitors are asked not to feed ponies. Doing so attracts them to roads, which may prove disastrous to them and to travellers, especially on dark, foggy winter nights. Ponies can also kick, and bite!

Princetown

Until the latter half of the 18th century the area now occupied by Princetown was still open moorland, unenclosed and grazed by the stock of farmers with common rights. At around 430 m above sea level, it is one of the most weather-beaten locations on Dartmoor, exposed to westerly winds and to the rain, mists and snow they so often bring.

Thomas Tyrwhitt, its founder, was a friend of George, Prince of Wales (holder of the Duchy of Cornwall lands on the moor). He was an MP and later Lord Warden of the Stannaries. He and others were convinced that a better living, producing general economic advantages, was possible for moor dwellers. Having established himself at Tor Royal in 1785, at a time when the moor's turnpike roads were taking shape, he began development of the place he named Princetown in honour of his friend and patron. Cottages were built, as well as an inn – the Plume of Feathers.

Following his plans for farming, forestry and quarrying, Tyrwhitt had the idea of building a prison at Princetown, as a way of housing

Dartmoor Prison at Princetown was originally built to house French prisoners-of-war during the Napoleonic wars

Princetown, and the transmitting mast on North Hessary Tor

large numbers of French prisoners from the Napoleonic Wars who were currently being confined in overcrowded hulks moored at Plymouth. This would solve a problem, and their labour, he felt, could advance his schemes. With the Prince's blessing, work in building the prison started in 1806.

Installation of the French prisoners, and later Americans from the War of 1812, brought a spell of trade and some prosperity to Princetown.

When the war ended in 1815 the prison became empty. Undaunted, Tyrwhitt proposed further plans, this time for a horse-drawn railway which would carry down the moor's exportable products and bring up timber, coal, and lime and sea sand for land improvement. This materialised as the Plymouth & Dartmoor Railway (see page 10).

Prince-town, nevertheless, fell into a period of depression until in 1850 the prison was re-opened as a civil prison, as it has remained, the mainstay of Princetown's commercial livelihood.

Stretches of land bordering the village, particularly to the north and east, have a more fertile, productive appearance than other areas of the high moor. This is largely because they are part of the Prison Farm. Between 1850 and 1870, land stretching from the prison to the Tavistock-Two Bridges road and beyond, amounting to 525 hectares out of a total grant of 800, was gradually improved by convicts.

Those farming at the prison had an advantage not available to ordinary moorland farmers – an abundance of cheap labour, and up to the early 20th century it was not uncommon to see perhaps two hundred prisoners at work on the land, setting drains, picking stones, and digging by hand. Although far fewer inmates are engaged in field work today, a high standard of hill farming is maintained, the whole still being held under lease from the Duchy of Cornwall.

Princetown continues to be dominated by the substantial grim, grey granite buildings of the prison, now much modernised since its earlier days. In two graveyards within the walls are buried the remains of French and American prisoners of war who died here in the early 19th century, and a short distance away across the road is the church of St Michael and All Angels, largely built by prisoners between 1810 and 1815 – the stonework by the French and the woodwork by the Americans.

The church has been the subject of recent renovation and restoration. There is also a prison museum which is open to the public. Fewer prison officers live at Princetown than in the past, many choosing to reside at Tavistock or elsewhere; some of their former houses have been demolished. Along the wide main street are a few small shops, cafés and pubs, while at the cross roads marking the village centre is an impressive building which in earlier times was the Duchy Hotel, then the prison officers' club, and is now the Dartmoor National Park Authority's High Moor Visitor Centre.

The former Duchy Hotel at Princetown

Artillery practice at Okehampton, about 1900

The Military

Dartmoor's expanse was used for small-scale military exercises, with occasional encampments, during the Napoleonic and Crimean Wars. Then, in 1873, major manoeuvres involving over 12,000 men and 2100 horses were held on Yennadon, Ringmoor and Roborough Downs. In 1875 the War Office, seeking space for artillery practice, examined the potential of the northern high ground. This appeared to meet requirements, so a licence was sought from the Duchy of Cornwall, and granted. In August that year a camp took shape in Okehampton Park and firing over 1200 hectares of the moor began.

Soon the camp functioned annually, initially for six weeks, and later for longer. A permanent camp was built, and the area extended, with firing almost daily from May to September. Flags flown warned the public, for whom the restrictions and dangers were of some concern. The arrangement brought advantages to Okehampton tradespeople, while farmers with common rights sought compensation for disturbance of grazing.

In 1900, during the war with South Africa, the War Office acquired a further 1300 hectares at Willsworthy, including Tavy Cleave, for a rifle and field-firing range. And soon, back at Okehampton, solid roads were being made on the moor for the increasingly mechanised military traffic.

At the start of the Second World War almost all of the area north of the Tavistock-Two Bridges-Moretonhampstead road became a firing range, and, in the south, Rippon Tor, Penn Moor and Ringmoor Down were subject to defence regulations for training purposes. Harrowbeer Airfield was established on Roborough Down. A camp was built at Plaster Down near Tavistock.

After the war there were soon calls for the release of the wartime restricted areas and for the land to be cleared of dangerous material. Following pressure and a public enquiry, the government decided that retained land should be reduced to about 13,500 hectares and the public given access on non-firing days.

The moor is still used for training, the Duchy's view being that its licence must accord with the defence policy of the government of the day. The Dartmoor National Park's objective is to seek termination of live firing and to minimise the impact of military activity on the environment.

The military authorities now give much attention to environmental protection and consideration for the public. A Dartmoor firing notice is published weekly in local newspapers and posted at public centres, showing firing dates on the Okehampton, Willsworthy and Merrivale ranges, when suitably sited warning red flags or lamps are hoisted.

Not all training involves firing, however. The rigorous elements provide challenging conditions for testing endurance, as does the terrain which, not dissimilar to that of the Falklands, served as a practice ground for many military personnel before that campaign.

Fire and manoeuvre on north Dartmoor

Railways

The coming of railways to Devon from the mid-19th century undoubtedly had an immense influence in bringing modernisation not only to the county as a whole, but also to Dartmoor. The arrival of the broad gauge Bristol & Exeter Railway at Exeter in 1844, and completion of the South Devon Railway to Plymouth in 1848, close to the moor's southern edge, were followed by other lines to carry people and goods nearer the moorland interior.

In 1859 a branch line to Tavistock was opened from a junction at Marsh Mills, just east of Plymouth, by the South Devon & Tavistock Railway Company. The line was extended (en route to Launceston) to Lydford in 1865. Here connection was made with the London & South Western Railway, coming around the northern edge of the moor via Okehampton, which reached Lydford in 1874 and eventually Plymouth. Dartmoor was thus virtually encircled by railways.

Bridestowe Station, on the London & South Western Railway line from Okehampton to Plymouth, as it was then (left) and as it is now (above)

In 1866 a line was opened from Newton Abbot to Moretonhampstead (a section near Bovey Tracey was constructed on part of the former Haytor Granite Tramway), and, in 1872, a branch from Totnes to Buckfastleigh and Ashburton. Also the upper section of the former Plymouth & Dartmoor (horsedrawn) Railway was reconstructed, with some deviations, and opened in 1883 as the Princetown Railway from Yelverton to Princetown, where its station was the highest on the Great Western Railway.

From the mid-20th century these lines were closed (apart from the main line south of the moor to Plymouth). An exception is the Totnes-Buckfastleigh line along the Dart valley which, known as South Devon Railway, has been developed as a tourist attraction. Others have been adapted as walking and cycling routes, while a 3 km length of the former L & SWR from Okehampton Station operates on Dartmoor's north-western slopes as Dartmoor Railway and carries visitors to the impressive Meldon viaduct – at an altitude of 290 m it was the highest point on the latter-day Southern Railway's system.

Burrator Reservoir seen from Ringmoor Down, one of Dartmoor's best known views. This reservoir has successfully merged with the landscape

Reservoirs

A modern development which has caused one of the greatest changes to Dartmoor's appearance has been the introduction of large reservoirs to serve the water needs of Devon's increasing population and industry.

Before the end of the 19th century, dams and reservoirs were constructed at Tottiford and Kennick on the moor's eastern fringe near Hennock, for supplying Torquay. A third, Trenchford, was built here in 1907. Meanwhile construction by Plymouth Corporation of Burrator Reservoir also proceeded. Flooding initially 47 hectares and impounding waters of the River Meavy, Burrator was completed in 1898. In 1928 the dam was heightened and the reservoir's area thereby increased to 60 hectares.

The growing town of Paignton called for a reliable water supply too, and early in the 20th century Venford reservoir was constructed on Holne Moor, to store waters of the Venford Brook. This was finished in 1907 and covers 13 hectares. The modern moorland road from Holne to Hexworthy is carried across its dam.

Torquay's continuing demands led to the building of Fernworthy Reservoir near Chagford, completed after some difficulties in 1942. It covers 31 hectares. Remains of ancient stone circles, and a bridge from the former trackway, may become visible in times of drought. After the war the newly formed South Devon Water Board created the Avon Reservoir on 45 hectares of moorland near South Brent – an area rich in prehistoric antiquities – which came into use in 1957.

Further supplies were still being sought by the North Devon Water Board, and after a prolonged period of controversy and objections the Meldon Dam impounded the tumbling waters of the West Okement in its previously wild and lovely valley. The Meldon Reservoir came into service in 1972. (Since then the much larger Roadford Reservoir was constructed some kilometres north of Dartmoor, which is expected to obviate further water problems in the foreseeable future.)

Fishing facilities are available on Dartmoor reservoirs: for trout at Kennick, Tottiford and Trenchford, Burrator, Venford, Fernworthy, Avon and Meldon, and for coarse fish at Trenchford. Information about this is available from South West Lakes Trust.

Smaller reservoirs and intakes also supply Dartmoor water for domestic and farm use.

One of these smaller reservoirs, on the site of the former Wheal Jewell tin mine on Kingsett Down near Mary Tavy, fulfils a different purpose: it provides power for generating hydro-electricity at a power station in Mary Tavy village. Holding water brought along leats from the River Tavy, the Wheal Jewell reservoir (SX 525813) has a capacity of over 27 million litres and the electricity produced is fed into the National Grid.

The Wheal Jewell reservoir, north of Mary Tavy, is a long, narrow reservoir. The water is used for generating electricity

The modern scene

And so it is clear that a number of factors have contributed to the making of modern Dartmoor. While much of the moor has remained unchanged, many of the activities it has supported over the last two hundred and fifty years have declined and disappeared, though some still survive, and a few have assumed greater importance.

One of the most prominent advances must surely be the development of communications. At the beginning of the period covered by this book, recognisable roads were being engineered across the moor from one side to the other. Gradually minor roads were also improved. By the dawn of the third millennium road surfaces were generally of a high enough standard to attract motor traffic of all kinds, though many remain as narrow lanes. Some routes have taken on rather too 'civilised' an appearance, with a proliferation of signs and white road markings, and a 40 mph speed limit (mainly to protect grazing livestock). The situation is very different from that less than a century ago when a journey across the moor presented the thrill of adventure.

The spread and general use of telephones have played an immense part in diminishing the former isolation of many moor dwellers. A notable and prominent addition to the scene is the transmitting station and mast on North Hessary Tor near Princetown. It was erected in 1954 at an altitude of 509m, and is symbolic of easy contact for people in their homes with the outside world through radio and television.

The use of Dartmoor as a place for recreation began in the late 19th century, when the main railway lines and their branches enabled people from other parts of the country to come and stay at such places as Bovey Tracey, Moretonhampstead, Chagford, Lydford and Ashburton, all of which became 'fashionable'.

As the railways declined and road transport developed, motor vehicles increasingly took to the moors. After the First World War moorland excursions by charabancs (later known as 'coaches') became popular. Following the Second World War, and with the progressive ease of car travel, the number of day trip visitors grew vastly, as did pressures on the natural scene.

In 1951, following the passing of the National Parks & Access to the Countryside Act of 1949, 365 square miles (945 sq km) of Dartmoor were designated as a national park. The legislation charged authorities

with preserving and enhancing natural beauty for recreation, as well as catering for the needs of agriculture and forestry. (The land in the national park is not nationally owned but continues in the hands of individuals or bodies: the Duchy of Cornwall is the largest landowner.)

Since its creation the Dartmoor National Park Authority, based at Bovey Tracey, has operated according to legal requirements. It is involved in providing general policies on planning, employment, holiday development, mineral working, conservation and other matters, and a number of specialists are employed. An important function is the provision of information to local people and visitors, and information centres operate at strategic points in the area.

Many people now walk on the moor all the year round, often in large organised groups. An annual event is the Ten Tors expedition which involves great numbers of young people. There is also increasing interest in knowledge about the moor itself – its history, its archaeology, and its flora, fauna and ecology.

Recommended reading

Dartmoor, a new study, ed. Crispin Gill (David & Charles, 1970)
Tin mines and miners of Dartmoor, Tom Greeves (Devon Books, 2ed 1993)
The Dartmoor tin industry, a field guide, Phil Newman (Forest, 1998)
The Industrial Archaeology of Dartmoor, Helen Harris (Peninsula, 4ed 1992)
The Haytor granite tramway and Stover Canal, Helen Harris (Peninsula, 2ed 2002)

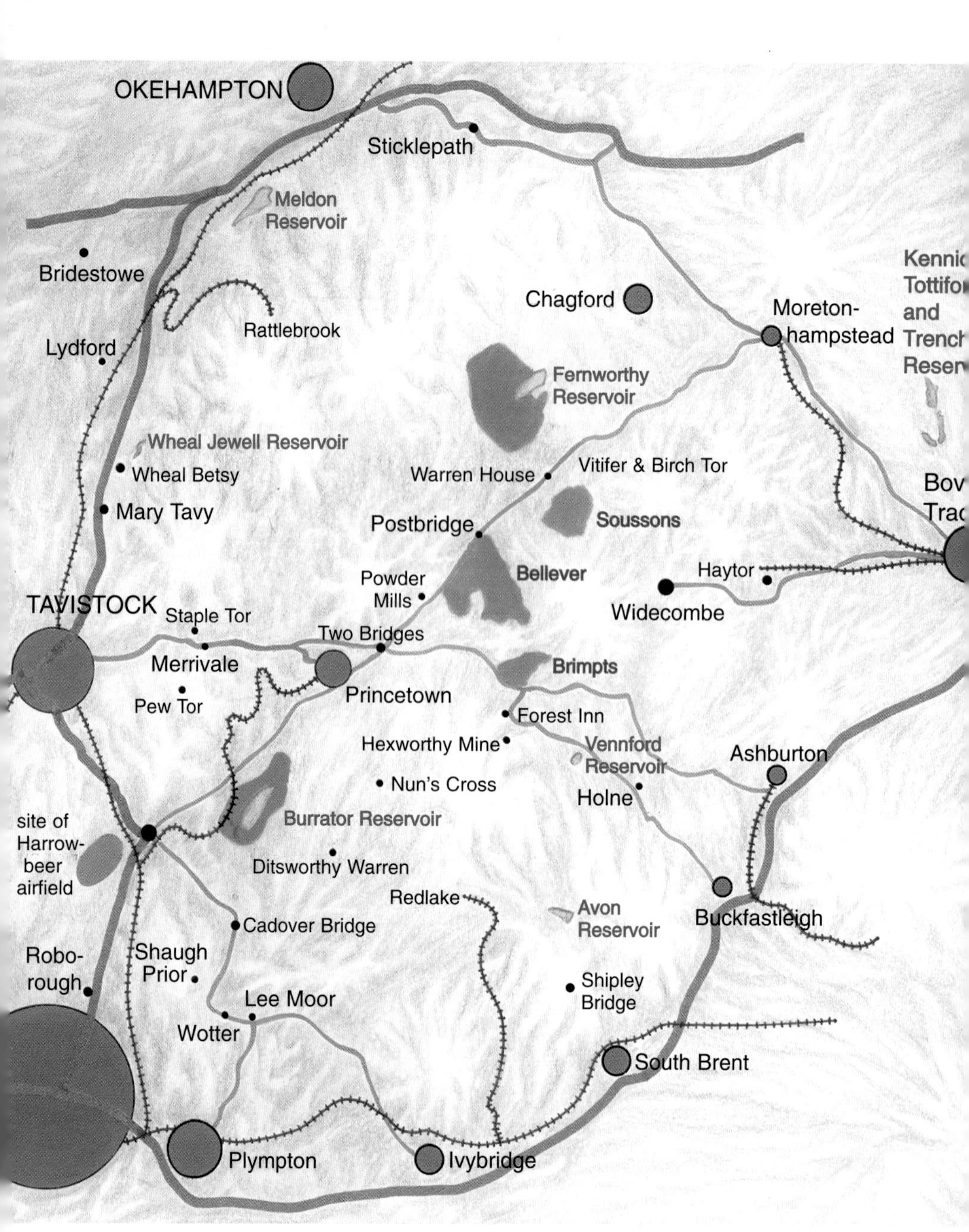

A composite map of Dartmoor in the 19th and 20th centuries. Some of the railways and tramways shown had already gone out of use before the major forestry plantations (green type) and reservoirs (blue type) were created